IN RECITAL®
with Christmas Favorites

ABOUT THE SERIES • A NOTE TO THE TEACHER

In Recital® with Christmas Favorites is devoted to wonderful Christmas repertoire. The fine composers and arrangers of this series have created engaging arrangements of timeless treasures, which have been carefully leveled to ensure success with this repertoire. We know that to motivate, the teacher must challenge the student with attainable goals. This series makes that possible while also providing a perfect holiday treat for your students. You will find favorites that are easy to sing along with, as well as recital-style arrangements of Christmas classics. You will also find some new Christmas gems. This series complements other FJH publications, and will help you plan student recital repertoire for holiday season recitals. The books include CDs with complete performances as well as "play along" tracks designed to assist with recital preparation. Throughout this series you will find a charming history of each Christmas carol researched by Miriam Littell.

Use the enclosed CD as a teaching and motivational tool. For a guide to using the CD, turn to page 40.

The editor wishes to thank the following people: Miriam Littell, for her superb research on the history of these Christmas carols; Kevin Olson and Robert Schultz; recording producer, Brian Balmages; production coordinators, Philip Groeber and Isabel Otero Bowen; and the publisher, Frank J. Hackinson, whose expertise and commitment to excellence makes books such as these possible.

THE
F·J·H
MUSIC
COMPANY
I N C.
Frank J. Hackinson

Production: Frank J. Hackinson
Production Coordinators: Philip Groeber and Isabel Otero Bowen
Cover and Interior Art Concepts: Helen Marlais
Art Direction: Terpstra Design, San Francisco
Cover and Inside Illustrations: Kevin Hawkes
Engraving: Tempo Music Press, Inc.
Printer: Tempo Music Press, Inc.

ISBN-13: 978-1-56939-490-8

ORGANIZATION OF THE SERIES
IN RECITAL® *WITH CHRISTMAS FAVORITES*

The series is carefully leveled into the following six categories: Early Elementary, Elementary, Late Elementary, Early Intermediate, Intermediate, and Late Intermediate. Each of the works has been selected for its artistic as well as pedagogical merit.

Book Two — Elementary, reinforces the following concepts:

- In addition to basic notes, such as quarter, half, dotted half, and whole notes, their corresponding rests are also used.

- Students play tied notes, *legato* and *staccato* articulations, accents, upbeats, a few chords, blocked intervals, and five-finger hand positions.

- Students continue to experience movement up and down the keyboard, and there is continuing use of the pedal to create a big sound.

- Pieces reinforce basic musical terminology and symbols such as *crescendo, decrescendo, diminuendo, poco ritardando, fermata, mezzo forte, mezzo piano, forte, piano, pianissimo, dolce,* and *D.S. al Coda.*

- Basic keys — C major, G major, F major, D minor, G minor (written using accidentals instead of key signatures) are used.

Many of the solos in Book Two have teacher accompaniments to enhance the overall sound of the piece. *Hark! The Herald Angels Sing* and *O Come, Little Children* were arranged as equal-part duets.

TABLE OF CONTENTS

ABOUT THE CAROLS

Christmas carols were introduced into church services by St. Francis of Assisi 900 years ago in Italy!

Assisi, Italy

Jingle Bells

If you were a student in Boston, Massachusetts in 1857, you would have been one of the first to sing this favorite Christmas song. The man who wrote the lyrics and the music, James S. Pierpont, named it *One-Horse Open Sleigh*, but the title changed to *Jingle Bells* after about two years. This is one of the best-known American Christmas songs, and probably the first! This song is so lively and happy that it is hard to imagine a Christmas season without this song or the sound of the sleigh bells that are often played with it.

We Three Kings of Orient Are

This Christmas carol tells the story of the three Wise Men who brought precious and rare gifts of gold, frankincense, and myrrh to the Christ child. John H. Hopkins, Jr. created the words and music in 1857, probably in New York City. The song was a big success with the composer's entire family. Its popularity spread, and it was soon published. This is probably the best-known song about the three Wise Kings.

Jolly Old Saint Nicholas

This bright and lively Christmas song is unique, because it is a highly popular American carol, yet nothing is known about the author. From its style we can determine that it was written in the United States, probably in the late 1800s or early 1900s. Some people think that Benjamin R. Hanby wrote it, because he wrote *Up On the Housetop*, and there are similarities between the songs.

FJH1574

Hark! The Herald Angels Sing

Charles Wesley was walking to church one Christmas morning in London, England in 1739, when he was inspired by the joyous ringing of the church bells to compose this carol. The melody was composed by Felix Mendelssohn in 1840 as part of a choral work, and an Englishman named William Hayman Cummings discovered the music and combined it with the words to create this famous Christmas carol. Have you ever wanted to create a song from something you heard? It took three people to create the carol we know today!

In Midnight's Silence (*Wsrod Nocnej Ciszy*)

The words and music to this song are of folk origin and were created in Poland, possibly 700-900 years ago! This is probably Poland's favorite carol. The Polish title is sometimes translated *In the Night's Stillness*. This lovely melody is often played in church at the stroke of midnight, as the lights are dimmed, to mark the beginning of Midnight Mass.

Over the River and Through the Woods

Can you imagine traveling through the woods in a horse-drawn sleigh? That was common in the time when this song was written, in the period between the Civil War and World War I (1865-1914). The carol is based on the poem, *A Boy's Thanksgiving Day* by Lydia Maria Child, in which the family travels "Over the river and through the woods, to Grandfather's house…" for Thanksgiving. The composer of the music is unknown. The poem has been adapted into a popular Christmas song, with the family going to "Grandmother's house."

O Come, Little Children

This song, a popular and beloved Christmas carol from Germany, from the 1800s invites children to come visit the manger and join in the miracle of Christmas Day. The words were created by a Catholic priest and schoolmaster who wrote children's literature and Bible stories. The words were set to a melody composed between 1787 and 1795 by J.A.P. Schulz.

Jingle Bell Hop

James S. Pierpont   arr. Timothy Brown

FJH1574

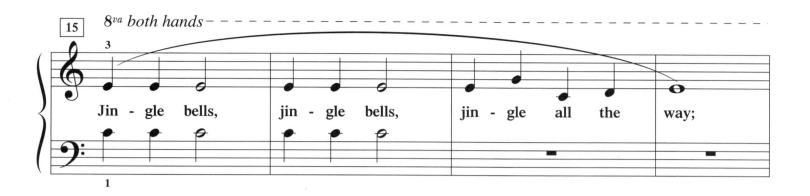

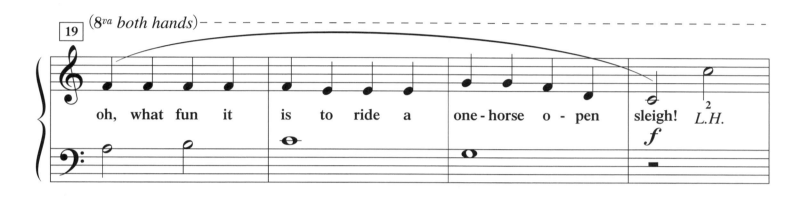

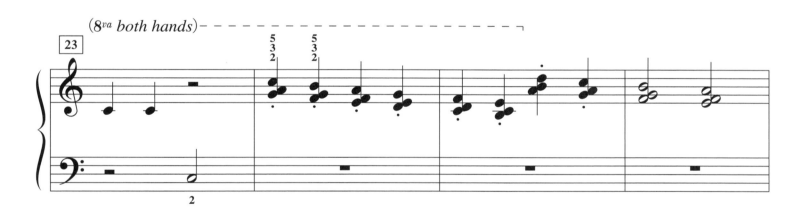

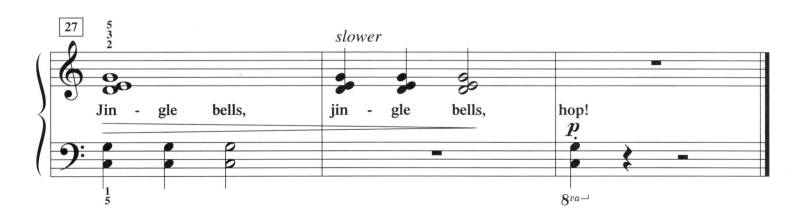

We Three Kings of Orient Are

John H. Hopkins, Jr.   arr. Edwin McLean

Teacher Accompaniment: (*Student plays one octave higher*)

FJH1574

Jolly Old Saint Nicholas

Traditional   arr. Kevin Costley

Moderately fast ($\quad$ = ca. 96)

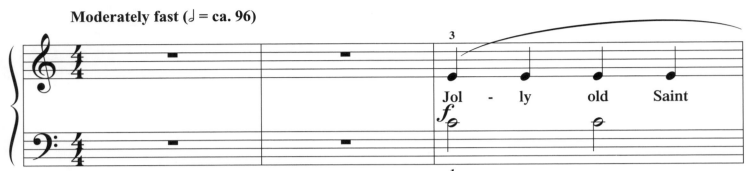

Jol - ly old Saint

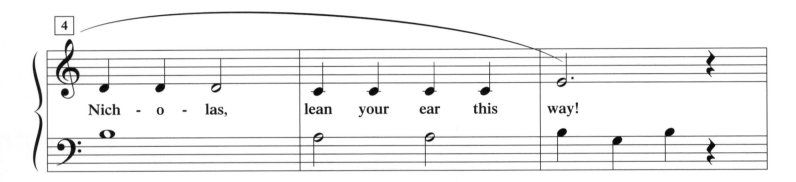

Nich - o - las, lean your ear this way!

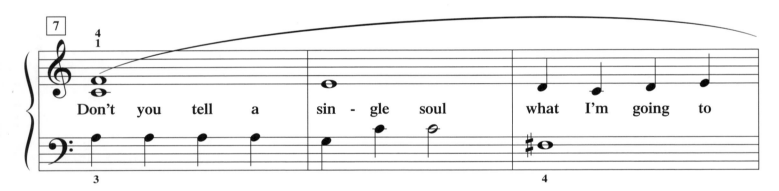

Don't you tell a sin - gle soul what I'm going to

Teacher Accompaniment: (*Student plays two octaves higher*)

FJH1574

Hark! The Herald Angels Sing

Secondo

Words: Charles Wesley   Music: Felix Mendelssohn   arr. Melody Bober

Triumphantly! (♩ = ca. 96-100)

Play both hands one octave lower

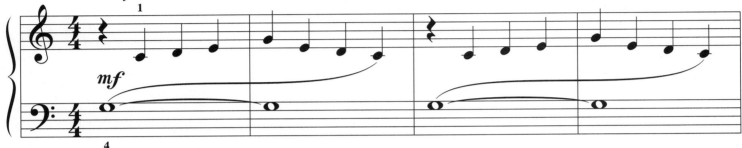

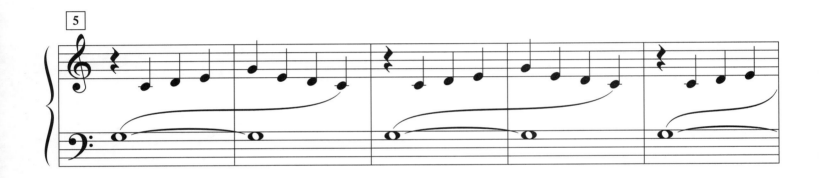

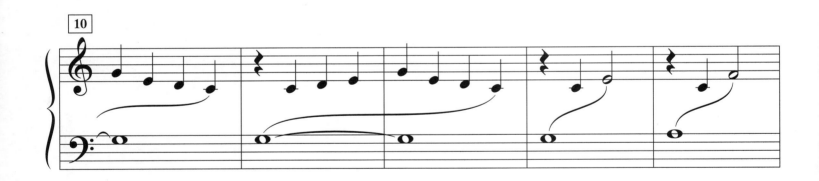

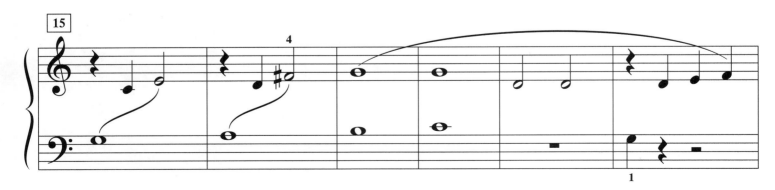

FJH1574

Hark! The Herald Angels Sing
Primo

Words: Charles Wesley   Music: Felix Mendelssohn   arr. Melody Bober

Triumphantly! (♩ = ca. 96-100)
Play both hands one octave higher

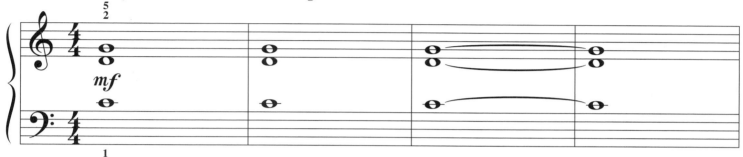

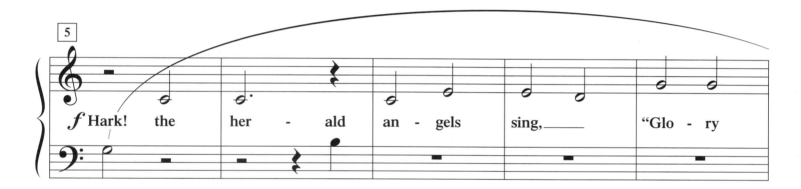

Hark! the her - ald an - gels sing,_____ "Glo - ry

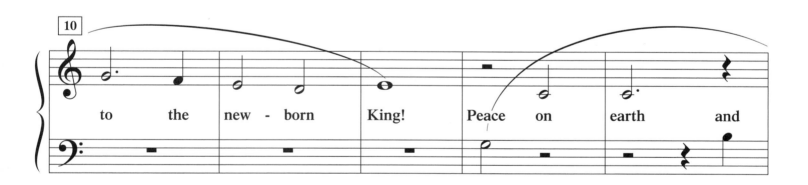

to the new - born King! Peace on earth and

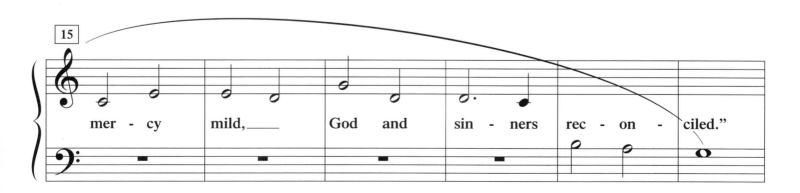

mer - cy mild,_____ God and sin - ners rec - on - ciled."

FJH1574

Secondo

Primo

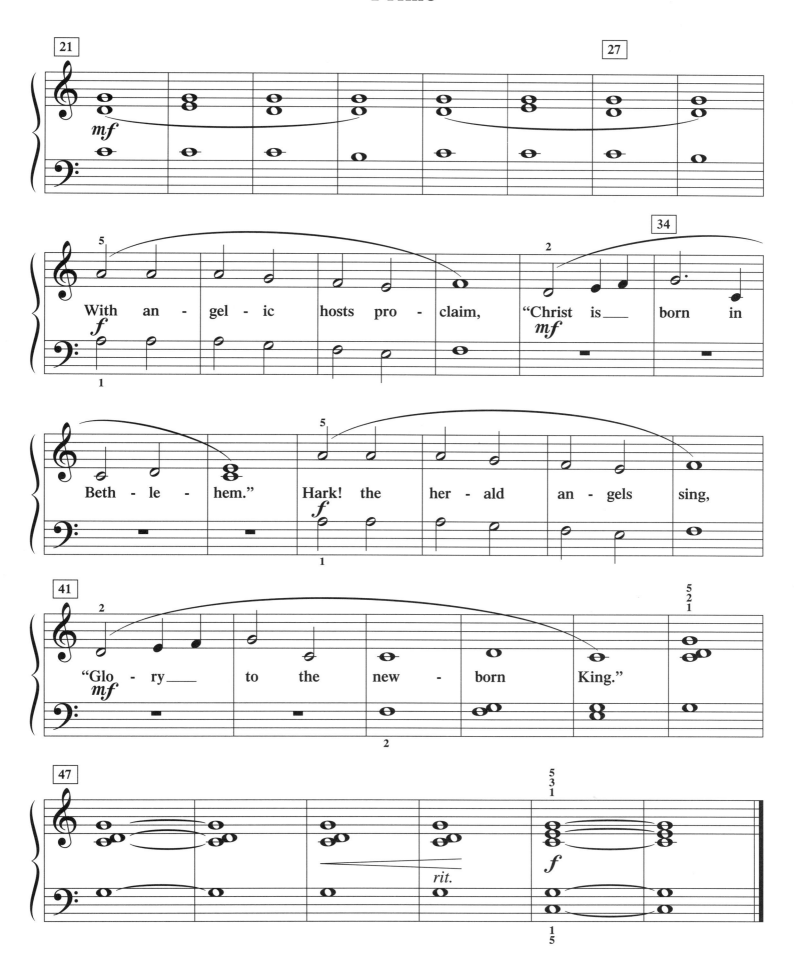

In Midnight's Silence
(Wsrod Nocnej Ciszy)
Teacher

Traditional Polish Carol   arr. Helen Marlais

FJH1574

In Midnight's Silence

(Wsrod Nocnej Ciszy)

Student

Traditional Polish Carol   arr. Helen Marlais

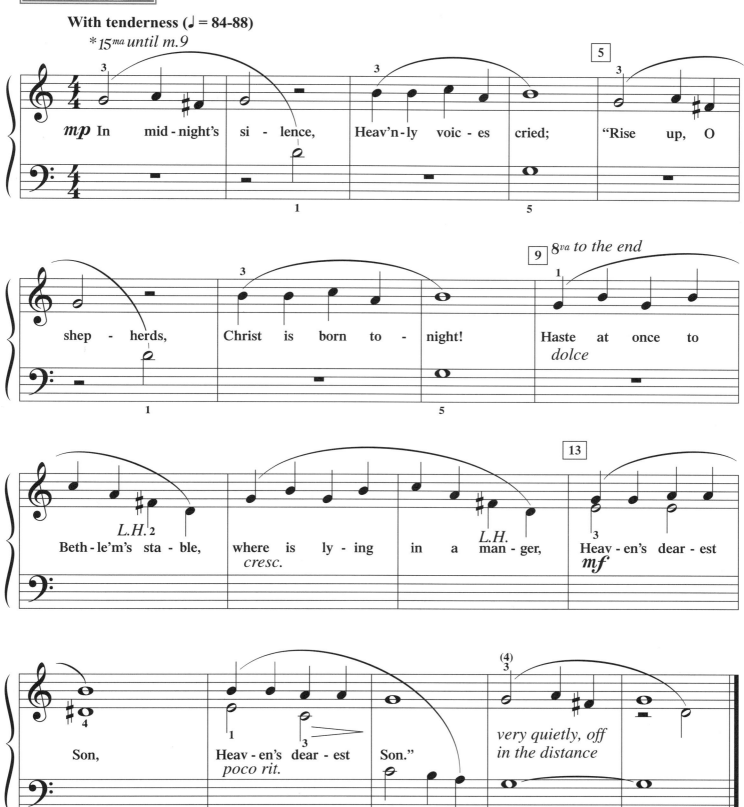

* *When playing as a solo, omit the 15ᵐᵃ and 8ᵛᵃ.*

Over the River and Through the Woods

Words: Lydia Maria Child   Music: Traditional   arr. Robert Schultz

O - ver the riv - er and through the woods to Grand-moth - er's house we go. _____ The horse knows the way to car - ry the sleigh through white and drift - ed snow. _____

FJH1574

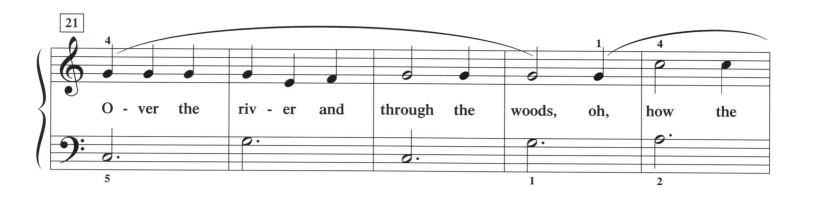

O - ver the riv - er and through the woods, oh, how the

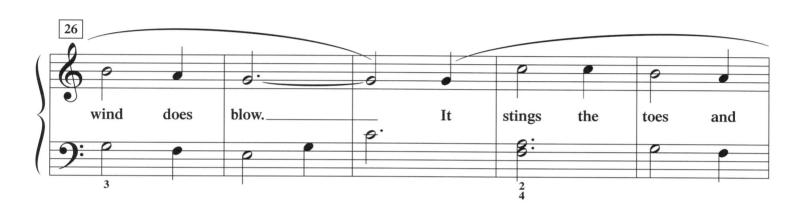

wind does blow. It stings the toes and

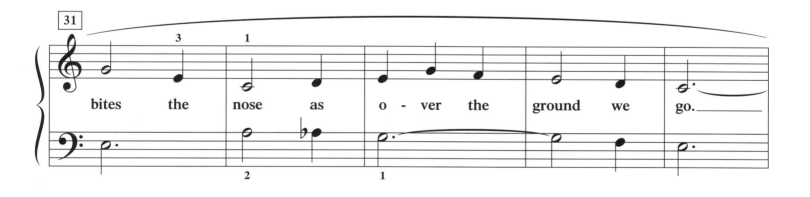

bites the nose as o - ver the ground we go.

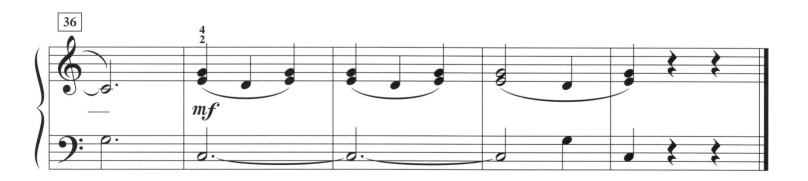

mf

O Come, Little Children
Secondo

Words: Christoph von Schmid   Music: J.A.P. Schulz   arr. Timothy Brown

Happily (♩ = ca. 112)

Play both hands one octave lower

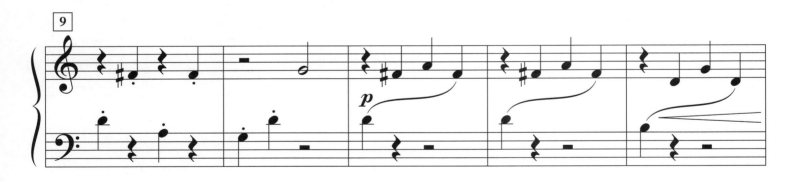

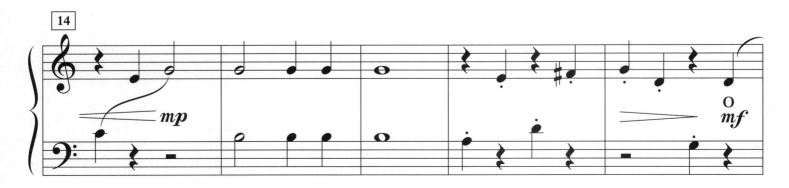

FJH1574

O Come, Little Children
Primo

Words: Christoph von Schmid   Music: J.A.P. Schulz   arr. Timothy Brown

Happily (♩ = ca. 112)

Play both hands one octave higher

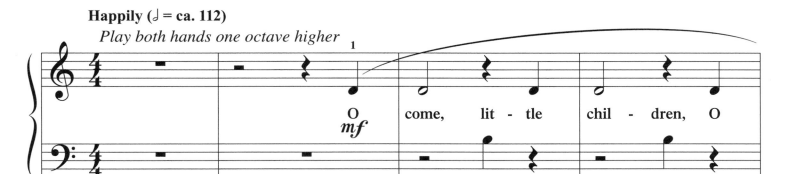

O come, lit - tle chil - dren, O

come, one and all, to Beth - le - hem haste to the

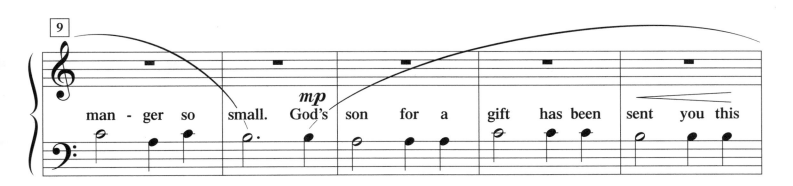

man - ger so small. God's son for a gift has been sent you this

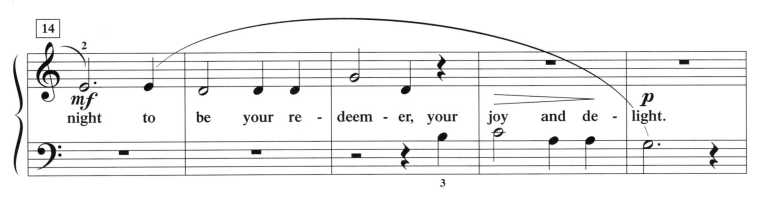

night to be your re - deem - er, your joy and de - light.

FJH1574

Secondo

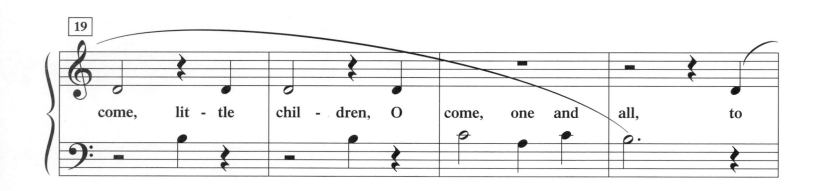

come, lit - tle chil - dren, O come, one and all, to

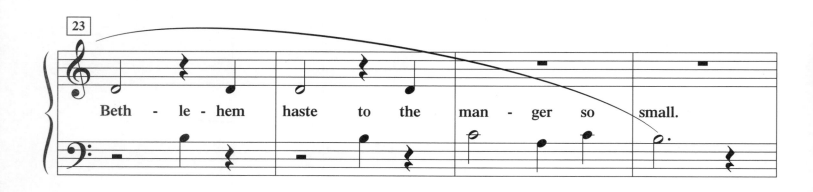

Beth - le - hem haste to the man - ger so small.

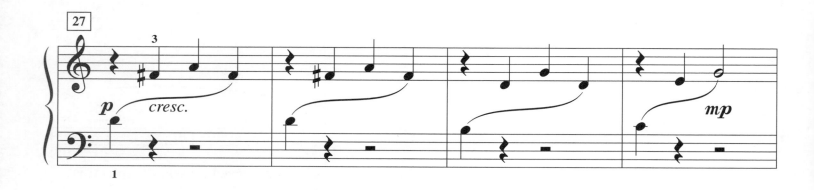

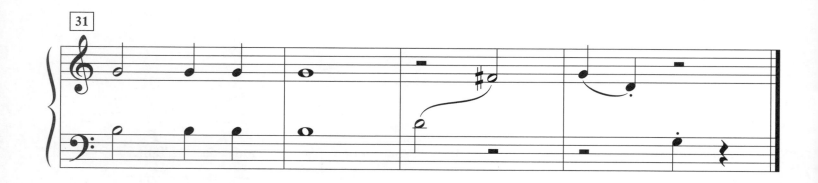

FJH1574

Primo

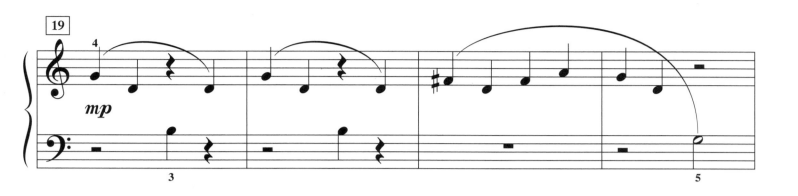

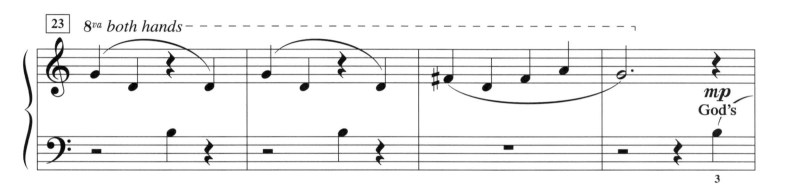

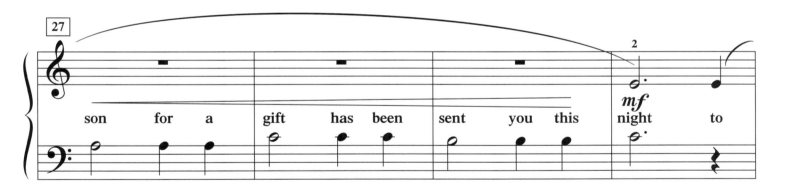

son   for   a   gift   has   been   sent   you   this   night   to

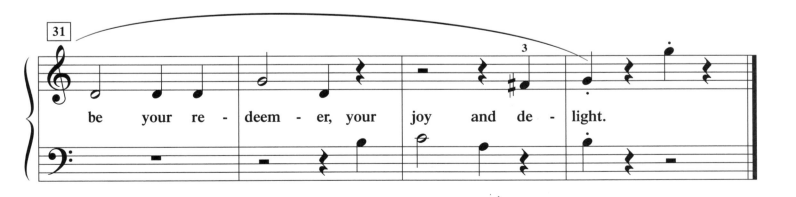

be   your   re - deem - er,   your   joy   and   de - light.

O Little Town of Bethlehem

Words: Phillips Brooks   Music: Lewis H. Redner   arr. Kevin Olson

FJH1574

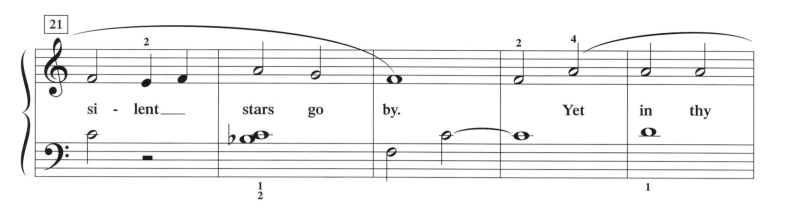

si - lent___ stars go by. Yet in thy

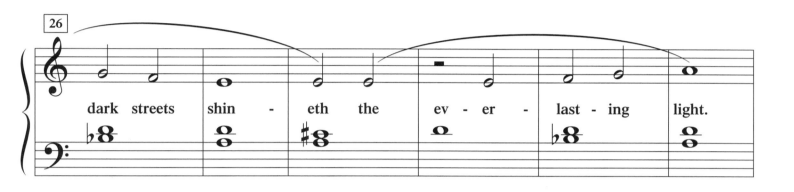

dark streets shin - eth the ev - er - last - ing light.

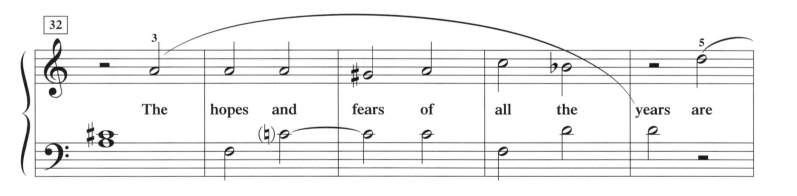

The hopes and fears of all the years are

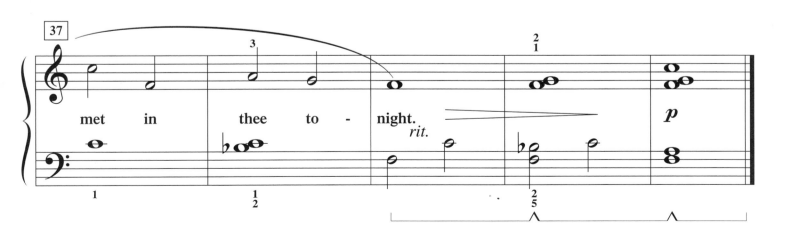

met in thee to - night. *rit.* *p*

Sussex Carol

Traditional English Carol   arr. Timothy Brown

Moderato (♩. = ca. 84)

On Christ-mas night all Chris - tians sing, to hear the news___ the an - gels bring. On Christ - mas night all Chris - tians sing, to hear the news___ the

Teacher Accompaniment: (*Student plays one octave higher*)

FJH1574

It Came Upon the Midnight Clear

Words: Edmund H. Sears   Music: Richard S. Willis   arr. Kevin Costley

FJH1574

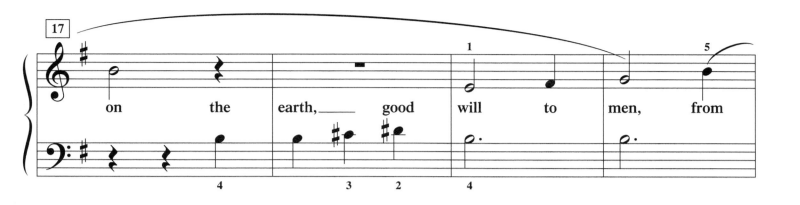

on the earth,____ good will to men, from

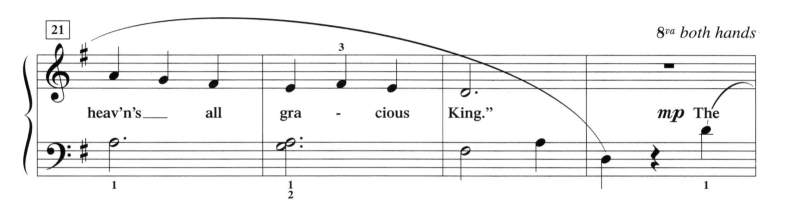

heav'n's____ all gra - cious King." *mp* The

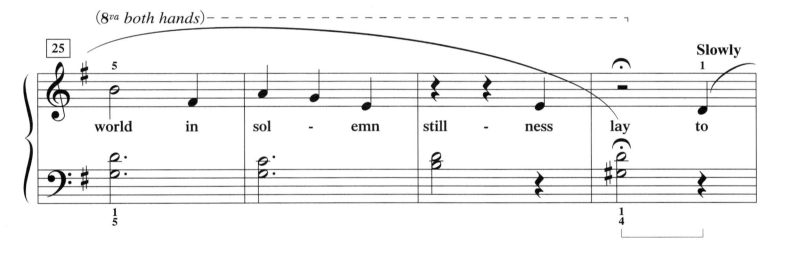

(*8va both hands*)- - - - - - - - - - - - - - - - -

Slowly

world in sol - emn still - ness lay to

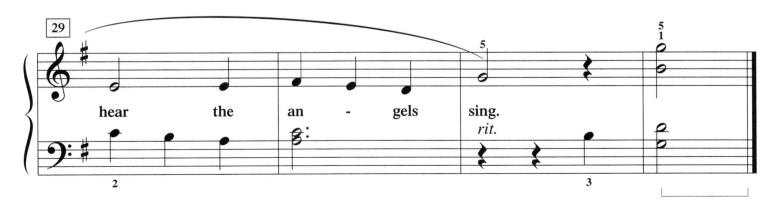

hear the an - gels sing.
rit.

Toyland

Words: Glen MacDonough   Music: Victor Herbert   arr. Robert Schultz

Flowing (♩. = 69)

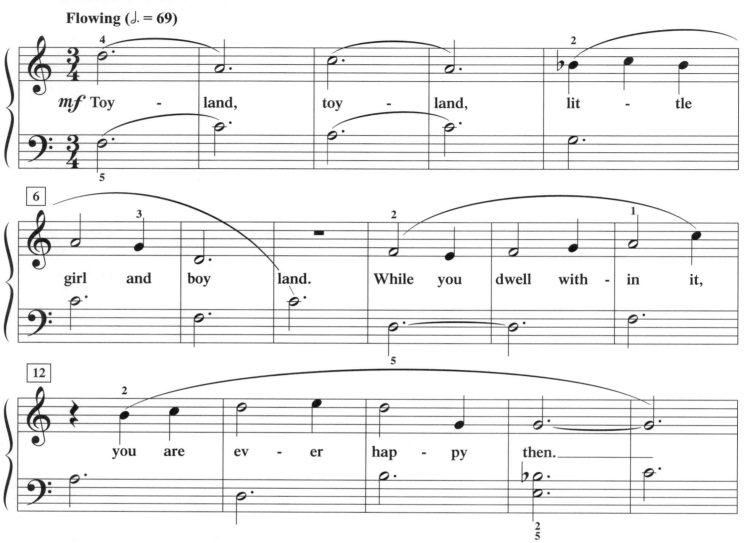

mf Toy - land, toy - land, lit - tle girl and boy land. While you dwell with - in it, you are ev - er hap - py then.____

Teacher Accompaniment: (*Student plays one octave higher*)

mp
with pedal

FJH1574

Sing We Now of Christmas

Traditional French Carol   arr. Kevin Olson

With spirit (♩ = 144)

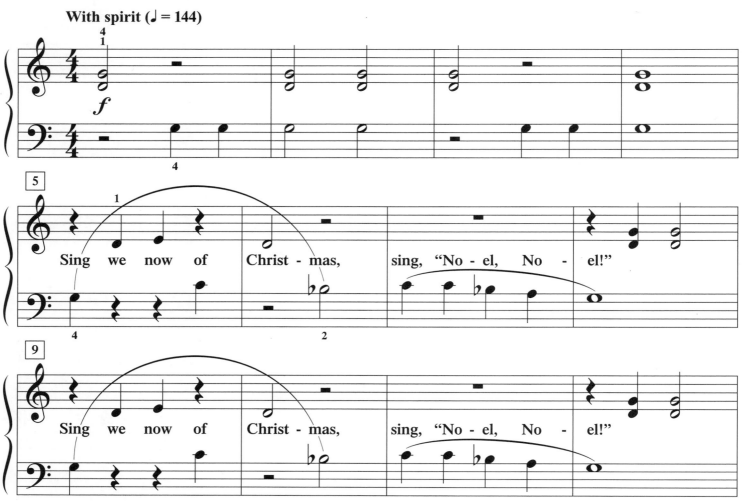

Sing we now of Christ - mas, sing, "No - el, No - el!"

Sing we now of Christ - mas, sing, "No - el, No - el!"

Teacher Accompaniment: (*Student plays one octave higher*)

mp

ped. simile

FJH1574

Go, Tell It On the Mountain

African-American Spiritual   arr. Melody Bober

FJH157

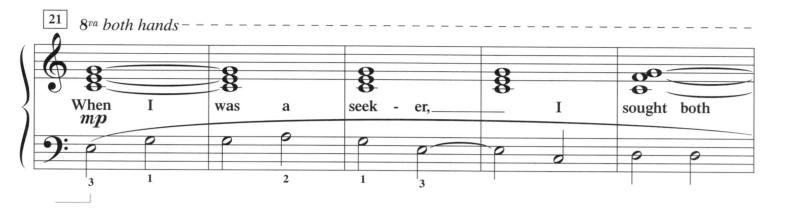

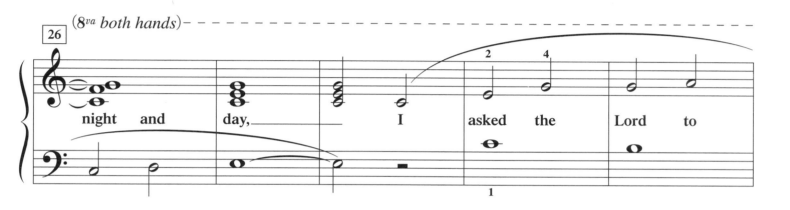

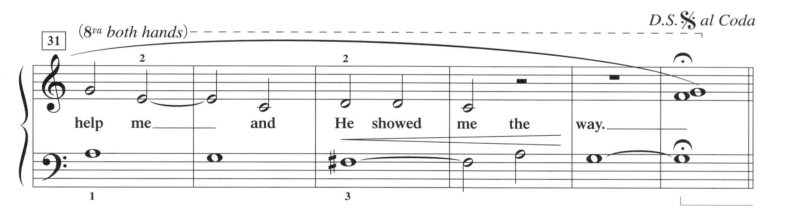

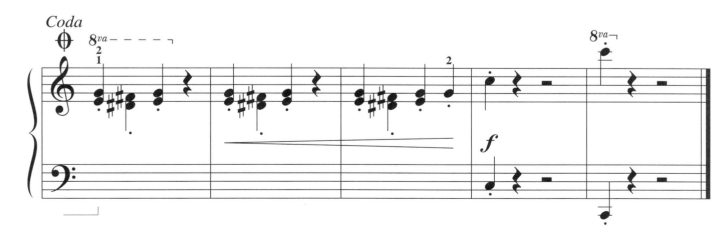

ABOUT THE CAROLS

O Little Town of Bethlehem

The words to this famous Christmas carol were written by Phillips Brooks, a minister from Philadelphia, Pennsylvania. He wrote the words in December, 1868, after a visit to the Holy Land when he went to a Christmas service in the Church of the Nativity in Bethlehem. The words were written for the Sunday school children to sing at his church's Christmas program. His friend Lewis Henry Redner, the church organist, wrote the music. The song was published in 1874.

Sussex Carol

The English have a passion for their Christmas carols. Practically no other nation has the carol accomplishments of England. The lyrics and music of this carol are of folk origin, and since the English have a unique custom of naming their folk carols after the places of their supposed origin, it is probably from Sussex, England. It was probably created in the eighteenth century. The first publication date appears to be 1842.

It Came Upon the Midnight Clear

This song was the first great American Christmas carol. The words were created by the Reverend Edmund Hamilton Sears in 1849 in Wayland, Massachusetts. The music was composed by a man named Richard Storrs Willis in New York City. Born to a prominent family in Boston, Willis had the opportunity to study music in Germany, where he made friends with the master composer Felix Mendelssohn. Willis chose one of Mendelssohn's pieces as the melody to this carol, and it was published in 1850.

FJH1574

ABOUT THE CAROLS

Toyland

This well-known song is from the 1903 operetta *Babes in Toyland*, written in the United States by the great Irish-American stage composer Victor Herbert, with Glen MacDonough writing the words. The spirit of the song is about the great pleasure that toys bring to children, and it represents the loving and giving that accompany the Christmas holiday. Maybe one day you will get the chance to see this small opera!

Sing We Now of Christmas

The Provence region of southern France is famous for its considerable contribution to Christmas carol literature. This is the region that produced *Bring A Torch, Jeannette, Isabella* and the lyrics to *O Holy Night*. During the Middle Ages, it was famous for wandering musicians, called "troubadours" who would travel from village to village, singing songs and playing instruments. The words and music to *Sing We Now of Christmas* were probably created in Provence about 400 years ago. Can you imagine being a troubadour singing this song and enjoying Christmas 400 years ago?

Go, Tell It On the Mountain

This African-American spiritual, probably created in the late nineteenth or early twentieth century in the United States, is a folk masterpiece. The African-American composer, scholar, and teacher Frederick J. Work and his nephew John Wesley Work carefully collected and preserved hundreds of African-American spirituals. Some think that this song, like many other spirituals, has an anonymous author, but John Wesley Work, who adapted the lyrics and arranged the music, attributed the writing of the song to his uncle.

Melody Bober

Piano instructor, music teacher, composer, clinician—Melody Bober has been active in music education for over 25 years. As a composer, her goal is to create exciting and challenging pieces that are strong teaching tools to promote a lifelong love, understanding, and appreciation for music. Pedagogy, ear training, and musical expression are fundamentals of Melody's teaching, as well as fostering composition skills in her students.

Melody graduated with highest honors from the University of Illinois with a degree in music education, and later received a master's degree in piano performance. She maintains a large private studio, performs in numerous regional events, and conducts workshops across the country. She and her husband Jeff reside in Minnesota.

Timothy Brown

Composition has always been a natural form of self-expression for Timothy Brown. His Montessori-influenced philosophy has greatly helped define his approach as a teacher and composer of educational music. His composition originates from a love of improvisation at the piano and his personal goal of writing music that will help release the student's imagination.

Mr. Brown holds two degrees in piano performance, including a master's degree from the University of North Texas. His many honors include a "Commissioned for Clavier" magazine article, and first prize award in the Fifth Aliénor International Harpsichord Competition for his solo composition *Suite Española*. As a clinician, Mr. Brown has presented numerous clinics and most recently represented FJH Music with his presentation at the 2000 World Piano Pedagogy Conference. Currently living in Dallas, Mr. Brown teaches piano and composition at the Harry Stone Montessori Magnet School. He frequently serves as an adjudicator for piano and composition contests, and performs with his wife as duo-pianists.

Kevin Costley

Kevin Costley holds several graduate degrees in the areas of elementary education and piano pedagogy, and literature, including a doctorate from Kansas State University. For nearly two decades, he was owner and director of The Keyboard Academy, specializing in innovative small group instruction. Kevin served for several years as head of the music department and on the keyboard faculty of Messenger College in Joplin, Missouri.

Kevin is a standing faculty member of Inspiration Point Fine Arts Colony piano and string camp, where he performs and teaches private piano, ensemble classes, and composition. He conducts child development seminars, writes for national publications, serves as a clinician for piano workshops, and adjudicates numerous piano festivals and competitions.

Helen Marlais

Helen Marlais has given collaborative recitals throughout the U.S. and in Canada, Italy, Germany, Turkey, Hungary, Lithuania, Russia, China, and England. She is recorded on Gasparo and Centaur record labels, and has performed and given workshops at local, state and national music teachers' conventions, including the National Conference on Keyboard Pedagogy and the National Music Teacher's convention. She is Director of Keyboard Publications for the FJH Music Company and her articles can be read in major keyboard journals.

Dr. Marlais is an associate professor of piano at Grand Valley State University in Grand Rapids, MI. She has also held full-time faculty piano positions at the Crane School of Music, S.U.N.Y. at Potsdam, Iowa State University, and Gustavus Adolphus College.

Edwin McLean

Edwin McLean is a composer living in Chapel Hill, North Carolina. He is a graduate of the Yale School of Music, where he studied with Krzysztof Penderecki and Jacob Druckman. He also holds a master's degree in music theory and a bachelor's degree in piano performance from the University of Colorado.

The recipient of several grants and awards: The MacDowell Colony, the John Work Award, the Woods Chandler Prize (Yale), Meet the Composer, Florida Arts Council, and others, he has also won the Aliénor Composition Competition for his work *Sonata for Harpsichord*, published by The FJH Music Company and recorded by Elaine Funaro (*Into the Millennium*, Gasparo GSCD-331).

Since 1979, Edwin McLean has arranged the music of some of today's best known recording artists. Currently, he is senior editor as well as MIDI orchestrator for FJH Music.

Kevin Olson

Kevin Olson is an active pianist, composer, and faculty member at Elmhurst College near Chicago, Illinois, where he teaches classical and jazz piano, music theory, and electronic music. He holds a Doctor of Education degree from National-Louis University, and bachelor's and master's degrees in music composition and theory from Brigham Young University. Before teaching at Elmhurst College, he held a visiting professor position at Humboldt State University in California.

A native of Utah, Kevin began composing at the age of five. When he was twelve, his composition *An American Trainride* received the Overall First Prize at the 1983 National PTA Convention in Albuquerque, New Mexico. Since then, he has been a composer-in-residence at the National Conference on Piano Pedagogy and has written music for the American Piano Quartet, Chicago a cappella, the Rich Matteson Jazz Festival, among others. Kevin maintains a large piano studio, teaching students of a variety of ages and abilities. Many of the needs of his own piano students have inspired over forty books and solos published by The FJH Music Company Inc., which he joined as a writer in 1994.

Robert Schultz

Robert Schultz, composer, arranger, and editor, has achieved international fame during his career in the music publishing industry. The Schultz Piano Library, established in 1980, has included more than 500 publications of classical works, popular arrangements, and Schultz's original compositions in editions for pianists of every level from the beginner through the concert artist. In addition to his extensive library of published piano works, Schultz's output includes original orchestral works, chamber music, works for solo instruments, and vocal music.

Schultz has presented his published editions at workshops, clinics, and convention showcases throughout the United States and Canada. He is a long-standing member of ASCAP and has served as president of the Miami Music Teachers Association. Mr. Schultz's original piano compositions and transcriptions are featured on the compact disc recordings *Visions of Dunbar* and *Tina Faigen Plays Piano Transcriptions*, released on the ACA Digital label and available worldwide. His published original works for concert artists are noted in Maurice Hinson's *Guide to the Pianist's Repertoire, Third Edition*. He currently devotes his full time to composing and arranging, writing from his studio in Miami, Florida. In-depth information about Robert Schultz and The Schultz Piano Library is available at the Web site www.schultzmusic.com.

A great way to prepare for your Christmas recitals is to use the CD in the following ways:

1) The first 13 tracks are the solo piano performances of each Christmas carol. Enjoy listening to these pieces anywhere anytime! Listen to them casually (as background music) and attentively. Follow along with your score as you listen and after you have finished listening, you might discuss interpretation with your teacher.

2) The rest of the tracks are to help you prepare for your Christmas recitals. The CD can be used as a practice partner, because you can play along with the tracks! This is how it works: Each carol has two accompaniment tracks. The first accompaniment track is for practice. It is at a slower tempo so that you can learn to play with the accompaniment. You will hear your part along with the accompaniment. You can play hands separately or hands together. The second version of the accompaniment is the "performance-ready" track. It is *a tempo* and does not include your part. All it needs to make it complete is your piano playing!

In both versions, before the accompaniment begins, you will hear a steady beat for two measures so that you know the tempo.

All of the CD orchestrations were created by Dr. Kevin Olson on a Roland KR-7 piano.